SHEARER

GUITAR
NOTE
SPELLER

FRANCO COLOMBO, INC.
(Formerly G. RICORDI & CO. of New York)

FOREWORD

Some guitarists play mostly by ear and more or less by rote which makes the process of reading music extremely difficult, if not entirely impossible.

The easiest and quickest way to learn to play the guitar is by learning to read music.

The purpose of this "GUITAR NOTE SPELLER" is to *simplify* the process of learning the positions of the notes in music and on the guitar fingerboard.

To obtain most benefit from this book it should be studied in conjunction with "Classic Guitar Technique", by Shearer.

The study material presented here is in the same order as is customarily learned on the classic guitar.

This book may also be used in the study of the plectrum guitar.

Aaron Shearer

Washington, D. C.

THE CONCERT GUITAR

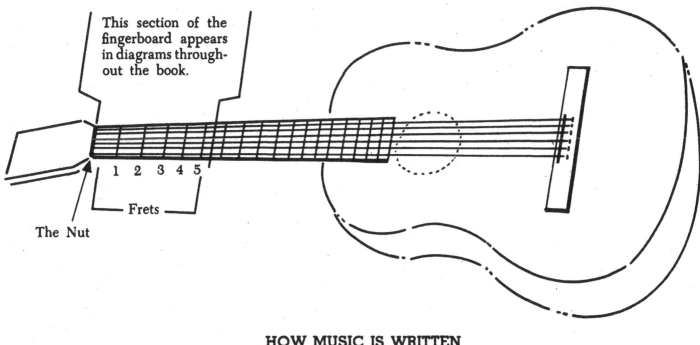

HOW MUSIC IS WRITTEN
(The Elements Of Notation)

1. a. Music is written on the STAFF consisting of five lines and four spaces numbered from the bottom upward, and b., on LEGER LINES and ADDED SPACES numbered outward from the STAFF:

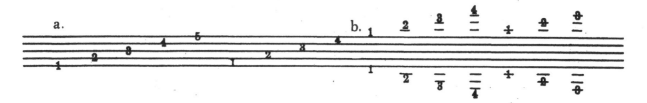

2. The TREBLE or G CLEF SIGN is placed on the staff so that the scroll encloses the second line establishing the position of the note "G". It is drawn in the following manner:

3. The first seven letters of the alphabet, A, B, C, D, E, F, and G are used to name the notes in music. The old aphorism, "Every Good Boy Does Fine" and the word "FACE", are excellent aids in memorizing the names of the lines and spaces:

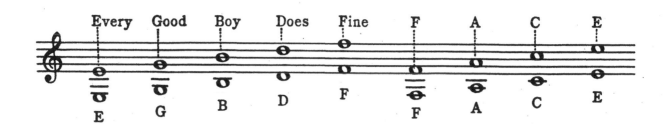

Notes of different TIME VALUE are used in writing music:

A WHOLE NOTE, **o** equals two HALF NOTES, ♩ ♩ or four QUARTER NOTES, ♩ ♩ ♩ ♩

THE OPEN STRINGS OF THE GUITAR

A string is said to be OPEN when no fret or left finger is used.

An "O" placed on or near a string means that the string is played *OPEN*.

THE FIRST THREE OPEN STRINGS
(E or 1st, B or 2nd, G or 3rd)

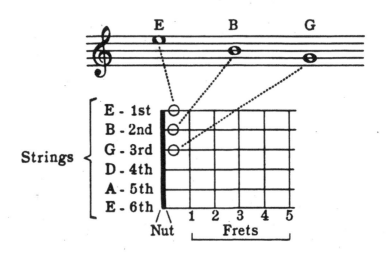

The OPEN 1st string E, is in the 4th space of the staff.

The OPEN 2nd string B, is on the 3rd line of the staff.

The OPEN 3rd string G, is on the 2nd line of the staff.

Write the LETTER NAME for each of the following OPEN STRING NOTES:
(This exercise is in QUARTER NOTES.)

E

Write the STRING NUMBER for each of the following OPEN STRING NOTES:
(This exercise is in HALF NOTES.)

Write the LETTER NAME *and* the STRING NUMBER for each of the following OPEN STRING NOTES
(This exercise is in WHOLE NOTES.)

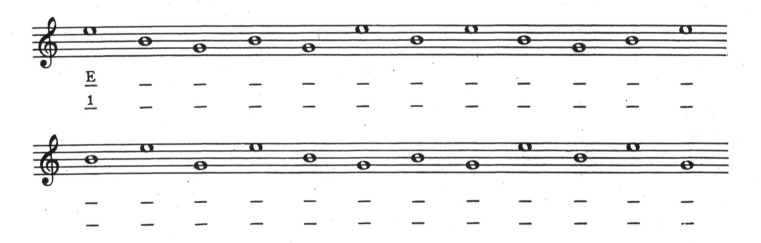

WRITING THE FIRST THREE OPEN STRING NOTES

Place a note on the staff and write the STRING NUMBER as directed by the LETTER NAME given below;
write WHOLE NOTES: **o**

Draw the TREBLE CLEF SIGN at the beginning of each staff.

1											
E	B	G	B	E	B	E	B	G	E	B	E

B	G	E	G	B	G	E	B	E	G	B	E

Place a note on the staff and write the LETTER NAME as directed by the STRING NUMBER given below; write WHOLE NOTES: **o**

Draw the TREBLE CLEF SIGN at the beginning of each staff.

E
1   2   3   2   3   1   2   1   2   3   2   1

2   1   3   1   2   3   2   3   1   2   1   3

THE 4th, 5th, AND 6th OPEN STRINGS

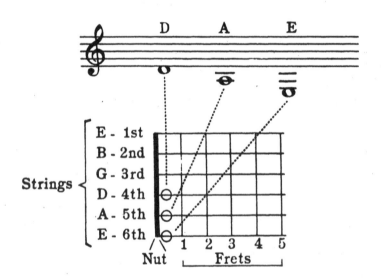

The OPEN 4th string D, is in the *first added space below* the staff.
The OPEN 5th string A, is on the *second leger line below* the staff.
The OPEN 6th string E, is in the *fourth added space below* the staff.

Write the LETTER NAME for each of the following OPEN STRING NOTES:

D   —   —   —   —   —   —   —   —   —

Write the STRING NUMBER for each of the following OPEN STRING NOTES:

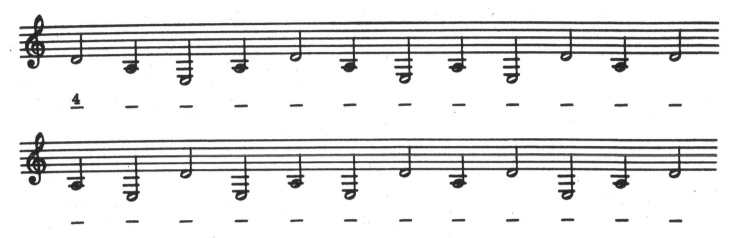

Write the LETTER NAME *and* the STRING NUMBER for each of the following OPEN STRING NOTES.

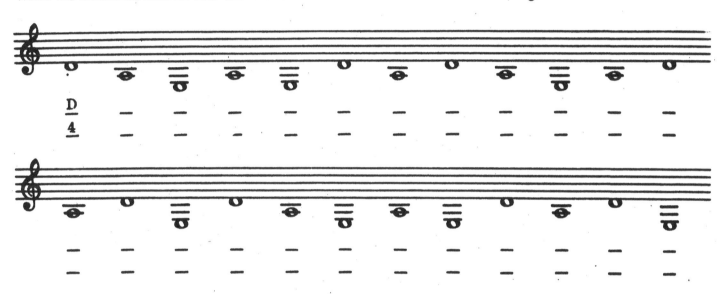

WRITING THE 4th, 5th, AND 6th OPEN STRING NOTES

1. Place the TREBLE CLEF SIGN at the beginning of each staff.
2. Write the following OPEN STRING NOTES as directed by the letter names, drawing LEGER LINES when necessary: make WHOLE NOTES: **o**
3. Write the correct STRING NUMBER for each note.

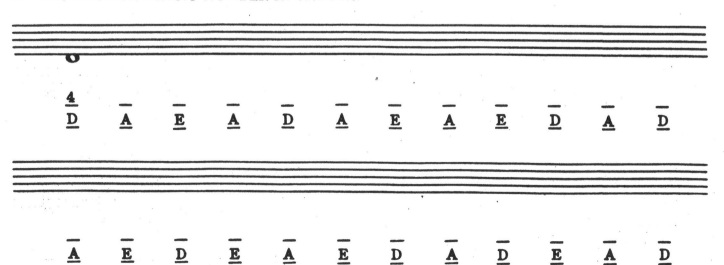

8

1. Place the TREBLE CLEF SIGN at the beginning of each staff.
2. Write the following OPEN STRING NOTES as directed by the STRING NUMBERS, drawing LEGER LINES where necessary; make WHOLE NOTES: **o**
3. Write the correct LETTER NAME for each note.

ALL SIX OPEN STRINGS

Write the LETTER NAME *and* STRING NUMBER for each of the following OPEN STRING NOTES.

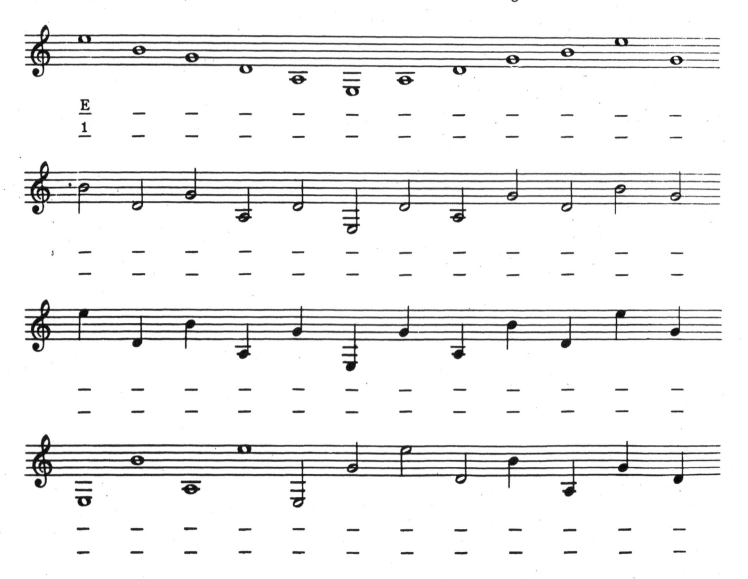

1. Place the TREBLE CLEF SIGN at the beginning of each staff.
2. Write the following OPEN STRING NOTES as directed by the STRING NUMBERS; drawing LEGER LINES where necessary; make WHOLE NOTES: **O**
3. Write the correct LETTER NAME for each note.

E
1   2   3   4   5   6   4   5   3   4   2   3

1   4   2   5   3   6   3   5   2   4   1   6

E-1st STRING NOTES
(E, Open; F, 1st Fret; G, 3rd Fret)

A number by the DOT (just back of fret) indicates the FRET and FINGER which are ALWAYS THE SAME:

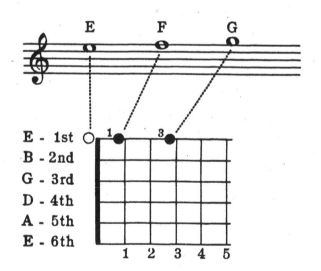

Write the LETTER NAME for each note:

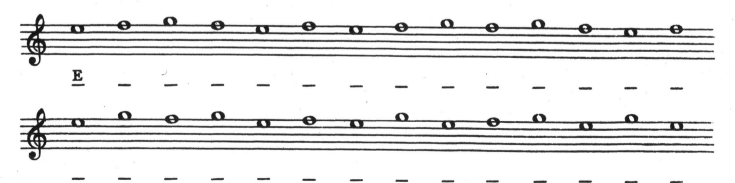

E

FC 1936

10

Write the FRET NUMBER for each note.
For the note "E", which is played open, write O

Write the LETTER NAME *and* the FRET NUMBER for each note; (O, for the Open "E".)

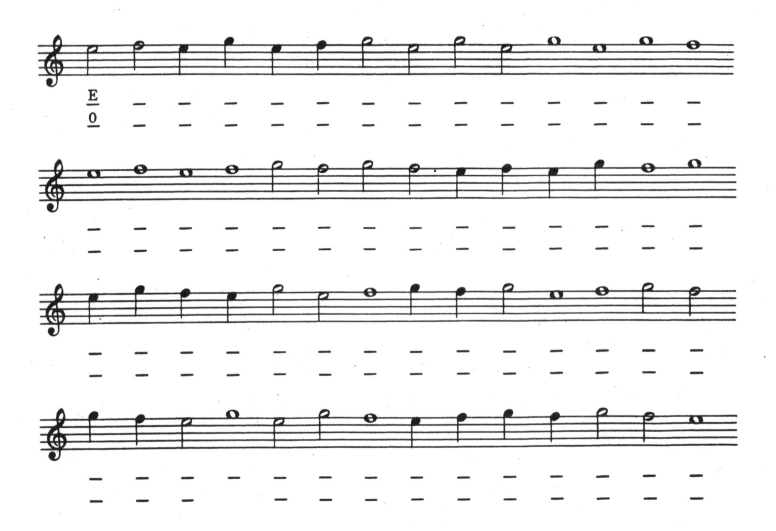

WRITING THE 1st STRING NOTES

1. Place the TREBLE CLEF SIGN at the beginning of each staff.
2. Write the notes as directed by the FRET NUMBER; make WHOLE NOTES: ○
3. Write the correct LETTER NAME for each note:

E
0 3 1 0 3 0 1 3 1 3 0 1 3 1

3 1 0 1 3 1 3 1 0 3 0 3 1 0

B-2nd STRING NOTES
(B, Open; C, 1st Fret; D, 3rd Fret)

A number by the DOT (just back of fret) indicates the FRET and FINGER which are always the same:

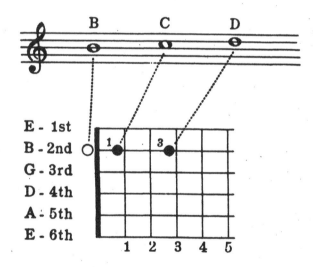

Write the LETTER NAME for each note:

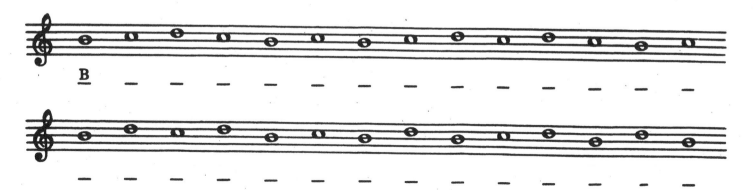

B

Write the FRET NUMBER for each note:

Write the LETTER NAME *and* the FRET NUMBER for each note.

1. Place the TREBLE CLEF SIGN at the beginning of each staff.
2. Write the note as directed by each FRET NUMBER; make WHOLE NOTES: **o**
3. Write the LETTER NAME for each note.

B
0   3   1   0   3   0   1   3   1   3   0   1   3   1

3   1   0   1   3   1   3   1   0   3   0   3   1   0

E-1st AND B-2nd STRING NOTES COMBINED

Write the LETTER NAME and FRET NUMBER for each note:

E
0   —   —   —   —   —   —   —   —   —   —   —   —

THE LETTER NAME — STRING NUMBER

Notes which have the SAME LETTER NAME but are located on SEPARATE STRINGS, (such as G on the 1st string and G-3rd Open) are often confusing at first. They are easily learned by writing the LETTER NAME and STRING NUMBER *TOGETHER;* E1, G1, G3, D2, etc., meaning E on the 1st string, G on the 1st string, G on the 3rd string, D on the 2nd string, etc.

E-1st, B-2nd, AND ALL OPEN STRING NOTES COMBINED

Write the LETTER NAME — STRING NUMBER and the FRET NUMBER for each note:

HOW TO WRITE NOTES WITH STEMS

1. When a note is BELOW THE MIDDLE LINE "B" OF THE STAFF its STEM is drawn on the RIGHT SIDE POINTING UPWARD:

2. When a note is ABOVE THE MIDDLE LINE "B" OF THE STAFF its STEM is drawn on the LEFT SIDE POINTING DOWNWARD:

3. The STEM of "B" on the MIDDLE LINE OF THE STAFF may point either UPWARD or DOWNWARD:

4. *Always* draw the STEM from its HIGHEST POINT DOWNWARD: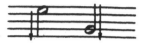

Draw the TREBLE CLEF SIGN.
Place a STEM on each of the following notes according to the rules just given.

In music for the guitar where two or more notes sound at the same time (harmonic music), stems of low notes usually point down, stems of high notes usually point up. The rules in items 1, 2, and 3 above, apply to all exercises in this book or when writing other single line (melodic) music. Item No. 4 is, of course, the correct manner of drawing a stem in any case.

WRITING E-1st, B-2nd, AND OPEN STRING NOTES

1. Draw the TREBLE CLEF SIGN.
2. Write each note as directed by the LETTER NAME — STRING NUMBER; make HALF NOTES: ♗ ♗
3. Write the FRET NUMBER for each:

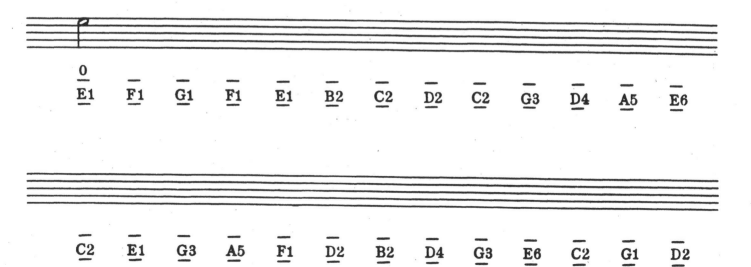

B2 E6 D2 D4 F1 A5 C2 G3 G1 E6 C2 F1 D2

D4 F1 G1 G3 F1 G1 D2 E6 G1 D2 C2 A5 B2

G-3rd STRING NOTES
(G, Open; A, 2nd Fret)

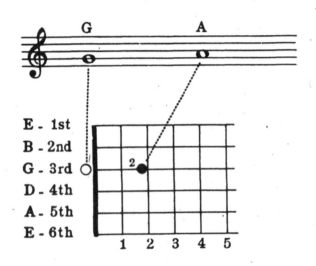

E-1st, B-2nd, AND G-3rd STRING NOTES COMBINED

Write the LETTER NAME — STRING NUMBER and FRET NUMBER for each note:

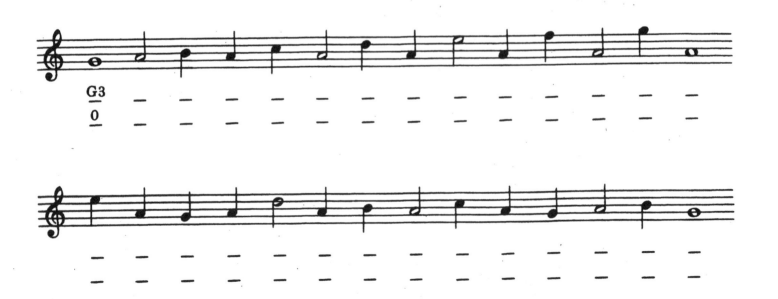

E-1st, B-2nd, G-3rd, AND ALL OPEN STRINGS COMBINED

Write the LETTER NAME — STRING NUMBER and FRET NUMBER for each note:

WRITING E-1st, B-2nd, G-3rd, AND OPEN STRING NOTES

1. Draw TREBLE CLEF SIGN.
2. Write each note as directed by the LETTER NAME — STRING NUMBER; make QUARTER NOTES: ♩♩
3. Write the FRET NUMBER for each:

E6   G1   D2   A5   F1   C2   D4   E1   B2   G3   D2   A3   A5   C2

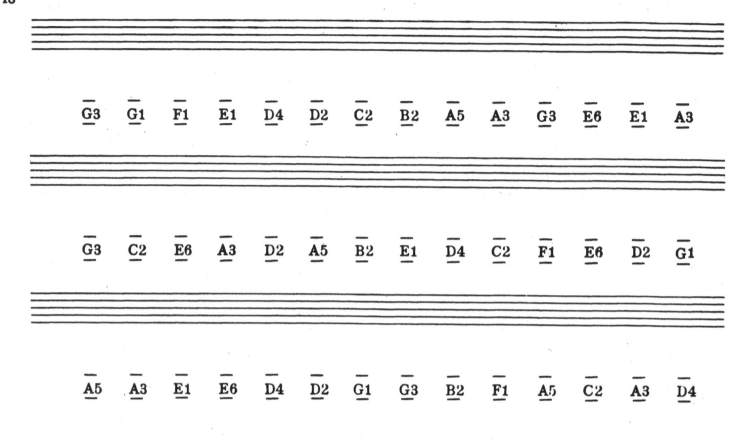

| G3 | G1 | F1 | E1 | D4 | D2 | C2 | B2 | A5 | A3 | G3 | E6 | E1 | A3 |

| G3 | C2 | E6 | A3 | D2 | A5 | B2 | E1 | D4 | C2 | F1 | E6 | D2 | G1 |

| A5 | A3 | E1 | E6 | D4 | D2 | G1 | G3 | B2 | F1 | A5 | C2 | A3 | D4 |

RECITATION EXERCISE
(Not To Be Written)

RECITE (Name Aloud):

1. The LETTER NAME — STRING NUMBER
2. The FRET NUMBER
3. The KIND OF NOTE (Whole, Half, or Quarter)

D-4th STRING NOTES
(D, Open; E, 2nd Fret; F, 3rd Fret)

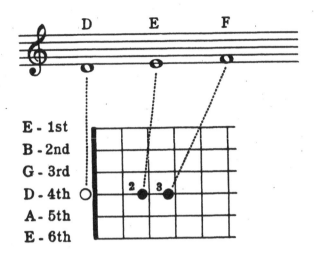

Write the LETTER NAME for each note:

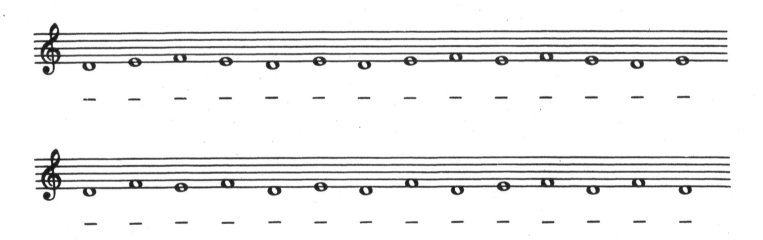

Write the FRET NUMBER for each note:

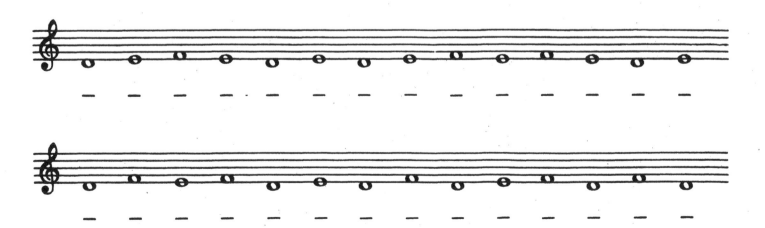

Write the LETTER NAME — STRING NUMBER and the FRET NUMBER for each note:

1. Draw TREBLE CLEF SIGN.
2. Write each note as directed by the LETTER NAME — STRING NUMBER; make HALF NOTES.
3. Write the FRET NUMBER for each:

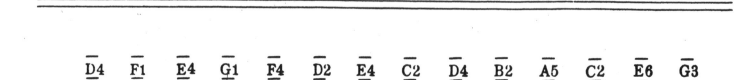

D4 F1 E4 G1 F4 D2 E4 C2 D4 B2 A5 C2 E6 G3

E̅4 A̅3 F̅4 D̅2 E̅4 G̅1 D̅4 F̅1 G̅3 E̅1 F̅4 D̅2 E̅4 C̅2

D̅4 D̅2 E̅1 E̅4 E̅6 F̅4 F̅1 G̅1 G̅3 A̅5 A̅3 E̅4 E̅6 E̅1

F̅1 C̅2 F̅4 E̅4 A̅3 E̅1 D̅2 B̅2 D̅4 A̅5 E̅4 C̅2 A̅3 F̅4

RECITATION EXERCISE

RECITE:

1. The LETTER NAME — STRING NUMBER
2. The FRET NUMBER
3. The KIND OF NOTE (Whole, Half, or Quarter)

A-5th STRING NOTES
(A, Open; B, 2nd Fret; C, 3rd Fret)

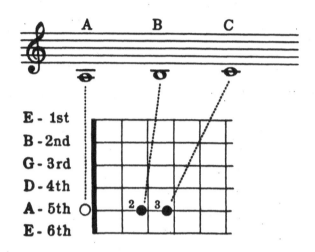

Write the LETTER NAME for each note:

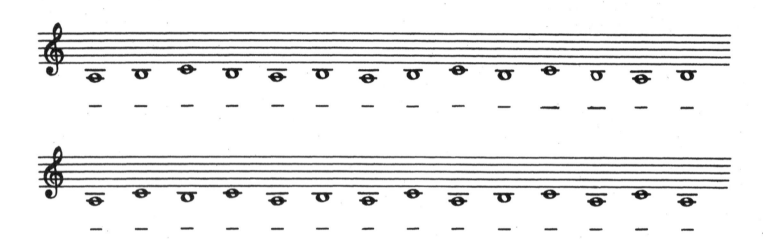

Write the FRET NUMBER for each note:

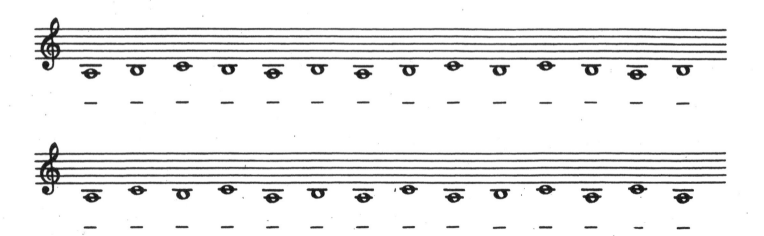

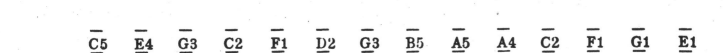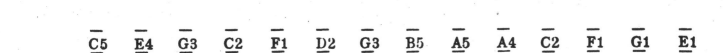

NOTES ON FIRST FIVE STRINGS WITH E-6th OPEN

Write the LETTER NAME — STRING NUMBER and the FRET NUMBER for each note:

1. Draw TREBLE CLEF SIGN
2. Write each note as directed by the LETTER NAME — STRING NUMBER; make QUARTER NOTES.
3. Write the FRET NUMBER for each note:

C5   E4   G3   C2   F1   D2   G3   B5   A5   A4   C2   F1   G1   E1

$\overline{B2}$ $\overline{D4}$ $\overline{C5}$ $\overline{F4}$ $\overline{A3}$ $\overline{D2}$ $\overline{F1}$ $\overline{B2}$ $\overline{D4}$ $\overline{E6}$ $\overline{B5}$ $\overline{G3}$ $\overline{D2}$ $\overline{C2}$

$\overline{A3}$ $\overline{A5}$ $\overline{C5}$ $\overline{C2}$ $\overline{E4}$ $\overline{E1}$ $\overline{D2}$ $\overline{D4}$ $\overline{B2}$ $\overline{B5}$ $\overline{F4}$ $\overline{F1}$ $\overline{G3}$ $\overline{G1}$

$\overline{F1}$ $\overline{F4}$ $\overline{E4}$ $\overline{E1}$ $\overline{D2}$ $\overline{D4}$ $\overline{C5}$ $\overline{C2}$ $\overline{B2}$ $\overline{B5}$ $\overline{A5}$ $\overline{A3}$ $\overline{E4}$ $\overline{E6}$

RECITATION EXERCISE

RECITE:

1. The LETTER NAME — STRING NUMBER
2. The FRET NUMBER
3. The KIND OF NOTE (Whole, Half, or Quarter)

E-6th STRING NOTES
(E, Open; F, 1st Fret; G, 3rd Fret)

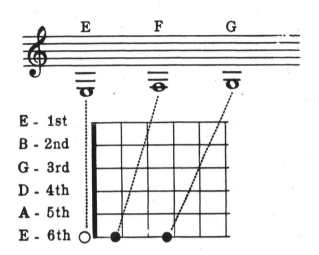

Write the LETTER NAME for each note:

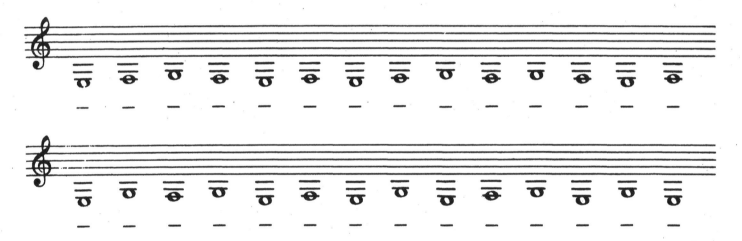

Write the FRET NUMBER for each note:

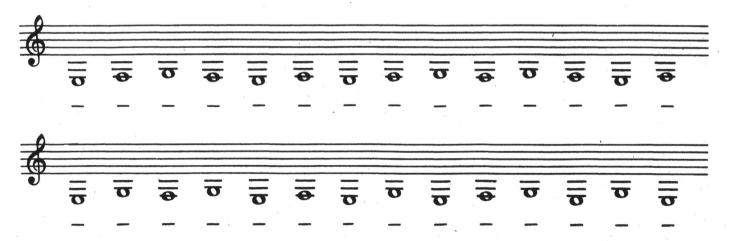

THE NOTES ON ALL SIX STRINGS

Write the LETTER NAME — STRING NUMBER and the FRET NUMBER for each note:

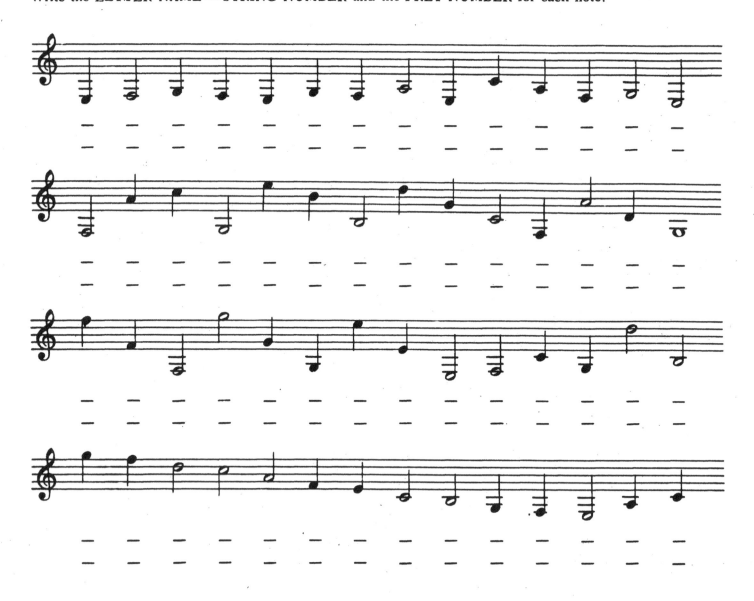

1. Draw TREBLE CLEF SIGN
2. Write each note as directed by the LETTER NAME — STRING NUMBER; make HALF NOTES.

F6   A5   C5   G6   B5   D4   A5   C5   F6   B5   D4   G6   C5   E4

$\overline{A}5$ $\overline{C}5$ $\overline{E}6$ $\overline{G}6$ $\overline{D}4$ $\overline{F}6$ $\overline{A}5$ $\overline{E}4$ $\overline{G}6$ $\overline{B}5$ $\overline{F}4$ $\overline{F}6$ $\overline{C}5$ $\overline{E}6$

$\underline{G}1$ $\underline{G}6$ $\underline{F}6$ $\underline{F}1$ $\underline{A}5$ $\underline{G}6$ $\underline{D}2$ $\underline{B}5$ $\underline{A}5$ $\underline{C}2$ $\underline{C}5$ $\underline{B}5$ $\underline{A}3$ $\underline{D}4$

$\overline{F}6$ $\overline{F}1$ $\overline{F}4$ $\overline{D}4$ $\overline{D}2$ $\overline{G}6$ $\overline{G}1$ $\overline{G}3$ $\overline{F}4$ $\overline{F}6$ $\overline{F}1$ $\overline{G}3$ $\overline{G}6$ $\overline{G}1$

RECITATION EXERCISE

RECITE:

1. The LETTER NAME — STRING NUMBER
2. The FRET NUMBER
3. The KIND OF NOTE (Whole, Half, or Quarter)

POSITION

POSITION on the guitar is designated by the FRET NUMBER upon which the 1st finger falls. The "First Position" means that the 1st finger plays the 1st fret notes, 2nd finger plays the 2nd fret notes, etc.

The following diagram shows the STRING and FRET NUMBER of each NATURAL NOTE in the FIRST POSITION. (Sharps # and Flats ♭ explained next section)

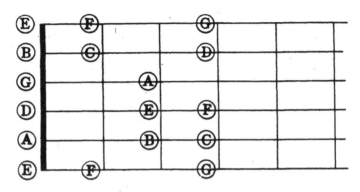

The following illustration shows the First Position notes written in ALPHABETICAL ORDER:

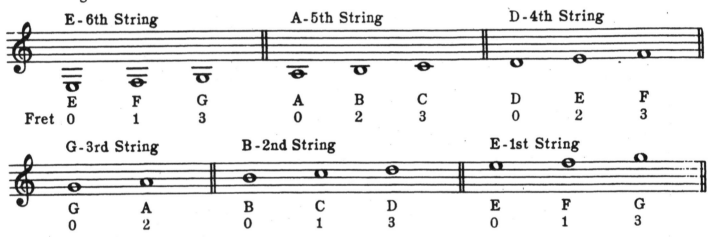

THE TWO FOLLOWING EXERCISES ARE OF UTMOST IMPORTANCE! The student must become thoroughly familiar with:

1. The PATTERN of NOTES PROGRESSING IN ALPHABETICAL ORDER.
2. The NAMES OF THE NOTES LOCATED STRAIGHT ACROSS EACH OF THE FIRST THREE FRETS.

THE NOTES IN ALPHABETICAL AND REVERSE ALPHABETICAL ORDER

Write the LETTER NAME — STRING NUMBER and the FRET NUMBER for each note:

NOTES ACROSS THE 1st, 2nd, AND 3rd FRETS

Write the LETTER NAME — STRING NUMBER and the FRET NUMBER for each note:

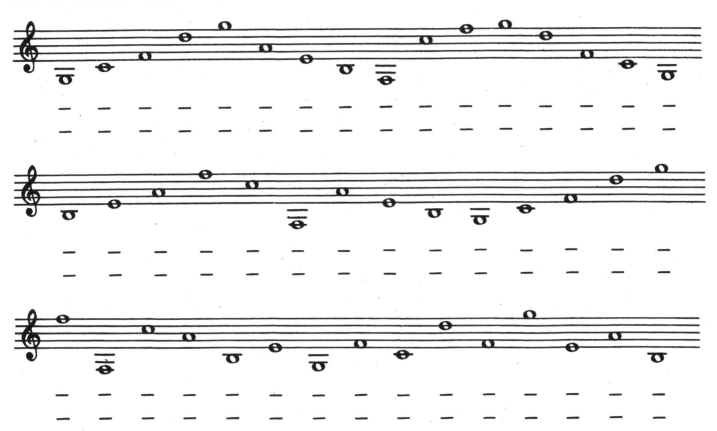

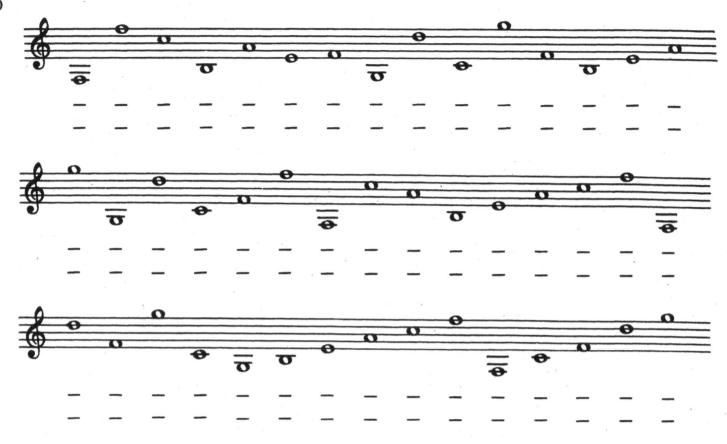

HALF AND WHOLE STEPS

A HALF-STEP is the distance from one note to the nearest note up or down; for example: from an open string to the first fret, or from any fret to the nearest fret either up or down. The following are HALF-STEPS:

A WHOLE-STEP consists of two half-steps; the following are the distance of two frets apart:

THE CHROMATIC SIGNS
(Also called ACCIDENTALS)

A CHROMATIC SIGN RAISES OR LOWERS its note one half-step. The following are the most commonly used Chromatic Signs:

The SHARP 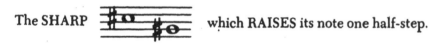 which RAISES its note one half-step.

The FLAT 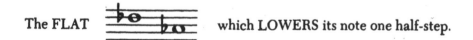 which LOWERS its note one half-step.

The NATURAL  which restores its note to the NATURAL pitch on the staff.

NOTES WITH CHROMATIC SIGNS
(Accidentals)

NOTES ON THE E-1st STRING	NOTES ON THE B-2nd STRING
(Open and first four frets)	(Open and first four frets)

The numbers 0, 1, 2, 3, 4, between the staffs indicate both fingers and frets.

From the above examples the student will observe that some notes are identical in position (and in sound) but have two names, for example: F♯ is G♭, D♭ is C♯, etc. In fact, any note which has a "sharp name" also has a "flat name" and vice versa.

ACCIDENTALS ON THE E-1st AND B-2nd STRINGS
(First Position)

Numbers in circles indicate strings.

Write the LETTER NAME and the FRET NUMBER for each note; letter names for sharps and flats are written: C♯, D♯, G♭, D♭, etc.

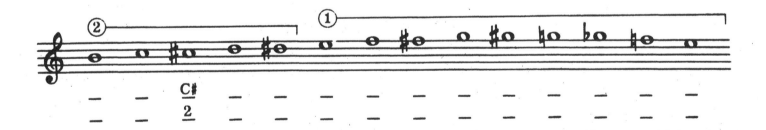

THE COMPLETE FIRST POSITION OF THE GUITAR
(In Half-steps)

Write the LETTER NAME and the FRET NUMBER for each note:

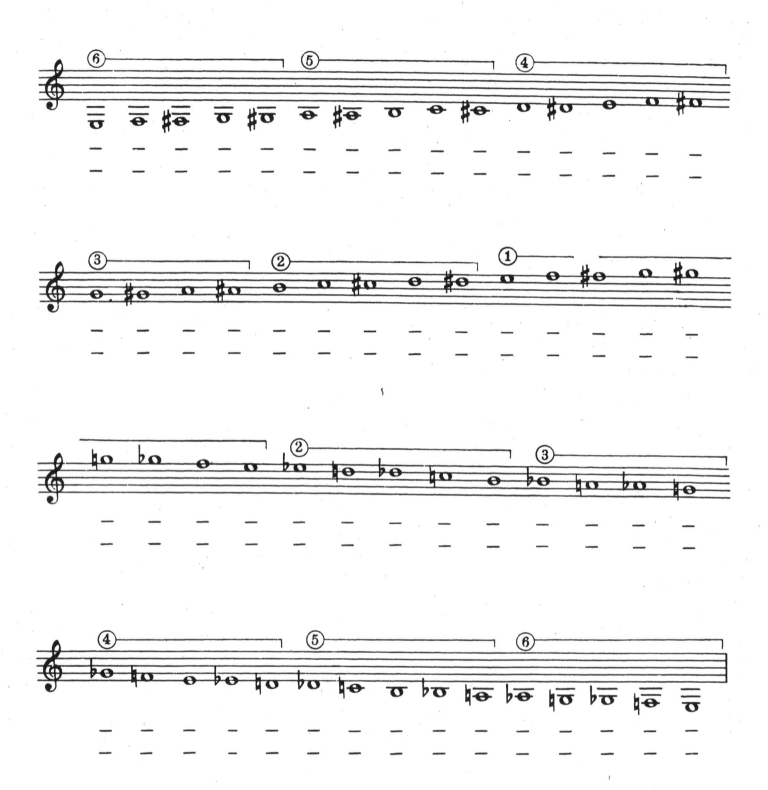

The foregoing section is not intended to represent a complete and thorough study of accidentals. It has been included in this work to merely acquaint the student with *ALL* the first position notes on the guitar fingerboard.